# THE ULTIMATE HANDBOOK

## VOLUME 3

By Mariah Balaban

SCHOLASTIC INC.

New York    Toronto    London    Auckland    Sydney
Mexico City    New Delhi    Hong Kong    Buenos Aires

ISBN-13: 978-0-545-03422-7
ISBN-10: 0-545-03422-1

12 11 10 9 8 7 6 5 4 3 2 1          7 8 9 10 11 12/0

Printed in the U.S.A.
First printing, December 2007

# TABLE OF CONTENTS

# AQUARIUM FRIENDS

Whether they're lounging on a rock or splashing around, these colorful critters are always up for some fun. Grab your snorkel and flippers and come join the party!

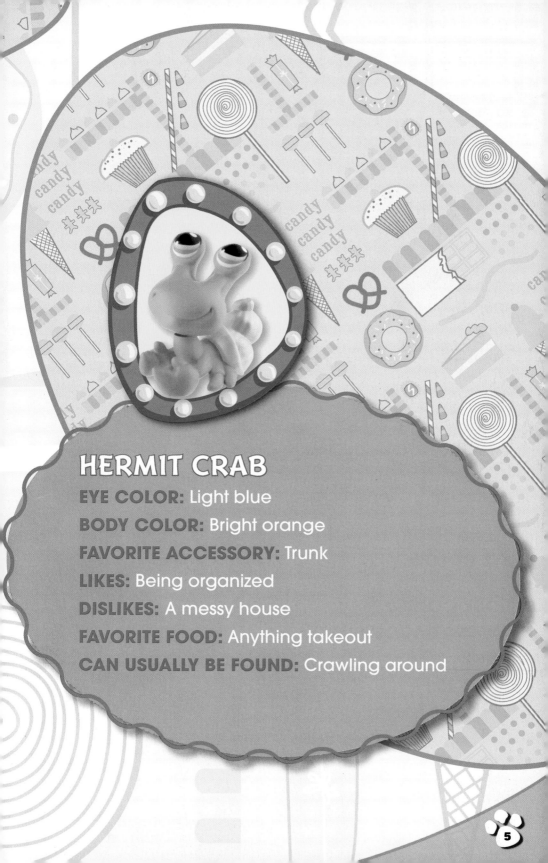

# HERMIT CRAB

**EYE COLOR:** Light blue

**BODY COLOR:** Bright orange

**FAVORITE ACCESSORY:** Trunk

**LIKES:** Being organized

**DISLIKES:** A messy house

**FAVORITE FOOD:** Anything takeout

**CAN USUALLY BE FOUND:** Crawling around

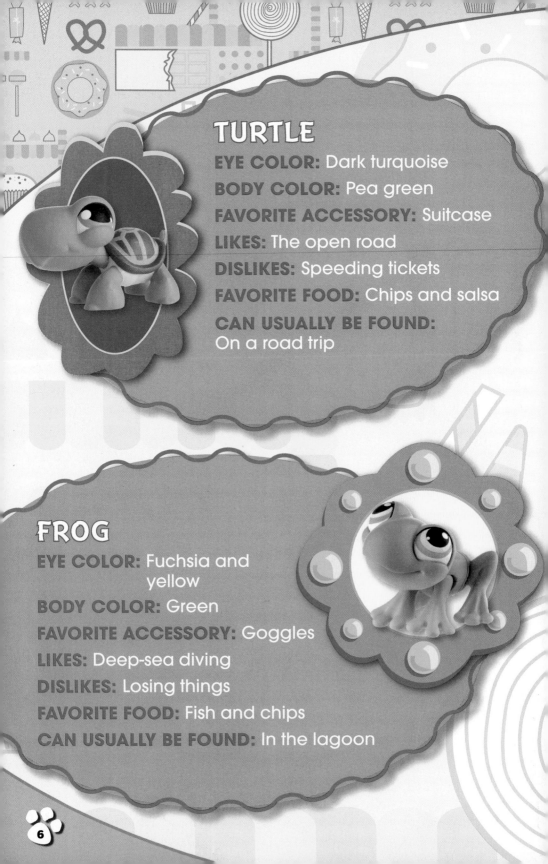

# TURTLE

**EYE COLOR:** Dark turquoise

**BODY COLOR:** Pea green

**FAVORITE ACCESSORY:** Suitcase

**LIKES:** The open road

**DISLIKES:** Speeding tickets

**FAVORITE FOOD:** Chips and salsa

**CAN USUALLY BE FOUND:**
On a road trip

# FROG

**EYE COLOR:** Fuchsia and
yellow

**BODY COLOR:** Green

**FAVORITE ACCESSORY:** Goggles

**LIKES:** Deep-sea diving

**DISLIKES:** Losing things

**FAVORITE FOOD:** Fish and chips

**CAN USUALLY BE FOUND:** In the lagoon

# DOG DAYS

There are rainy days and sunny days, but the most fun kind of days are dog days! So break out the chew toys and the doggy treats. These fluffy friends will be loyal until the end!

# CORGI

**EYE COLOR:** Light green

**BODY COLOR:** Golden brown

**FAVORITE ACCESSORY:** Surfboard

**LIKES:** Walks on the beach

**DISLIKES:** Jellyfish

**FAVORITE FOOD:** Tuna salad sandwiches

**CAN USUALLY BE FOUND:** Splashing in the waves

# GREAT DANE

**EYE COLOR:** Swimming-pool blue

**BODY COLOR:** Cocoa brown

**FAVORITE ACCESSORY:** Roller skates

**LIKES:** Rainbows

**DISLIKES:** Bumpy pavement

**FAVORITE FOOD:** Doughnuts

**CAN USUALLY BE FOUND:** At the roller disco

# BROWN DOG

**EYE COLOR:** Baby blue

**BODY COLOR:** Brown and tan

**FAVORITE ACCESSORY:** Pink tiara

**LIKES:** Reading fashion magazines

**DISLIKES:** Breaking a nail

**FAVORITE FOOD:** Salmon pâté

**CAN USUALLY BE FOUND:** Getting her hair done

# DOG

**EYE COLOR:** Bright blue

**BODY COLOR:** White and tan

**FAVORITE ACCESSORY:** A blue ribbon

**LIKES:** Being in first place

**DISLIKES:** Dogs that are cuter than him

**FAVORITE FOOD:** Filet mignon

**CAN USUALLY BE FOUND:** In the winner's circle

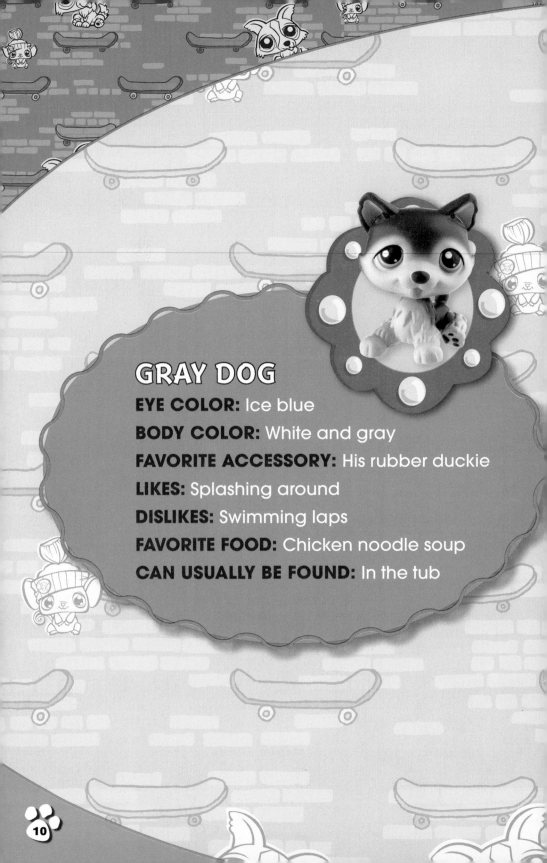

# GRAY DOG

**EYE COLOR:** Ice blue

**BODY COLOR:** White and gray

**FAVORITE ACCESSORY:** His rubber duckie

**LIKES:** Splashing around

**DISLIKES:** Swimming laps

**FAVORITE FOOD:** Chicken noodle soup

**CAN USUALLY BE FOUND:** In the tub

# DOG

**EYE COLOR:** Light blue

**BODY COLOR:** White and brown

**FAVORITE ACCESSORY:** Microphone

**LIKES:** Karaoke

**DISLIKES:** Singing backup

**FAVORITE FOOD:** Sushi

**CAN USUALLY BE FOUND:** On stage

# PUPPY

**EYE COLOR:** Light green

**BODY COLOR:** White

**FAVORITE ACCESSORY:** Pink bow

**LIKES:** Playing dress-up

**DISLIKES:** Getting dirty

**FAVORITE FOOD:** Angel food cake

**CAN USUALLY BE FOUND:** Playing with her dolls

# PUPPY

**EYE COLOR:** Light blue

**BODY COLOR:** White

**FAVORITE ACCESSORY:** Old chew toy

**LIKES:** Getting dirty

**DISLIKES:** Bath time

**FAVORITE FOOD:** Sloppy joes

**CAN USUALLY BE FOUND:** Rolling in the mud

# BOXER

**EYE COLOR:** Olive green

**BODY COLOR:** Light tan

**FAVORITE ACCESSORY:** Golf clubs

**LIKES:** Getting a hole in one

**DISLIKES:** Sand traps

**FAVORITE FOOD:** Turkey clubs

**CAN USUALLY BE FOUND:** Riding in a golf cart

# MAGIC MOTION

Whether it's a romp in the park or a spin around the dance floor, these pets are real movers and shakers. They're always on the go, so you'd better be fast if you want to keep up with them!

## BUNNY

**EYE COLOR:** Grass green

**BODY COLOR:** Brown and tan

**FAVORITE ACCESSORY:** A smile

**LIKES:** Helping her friends

**DISLIKES:** Being late

**FAVORITE FOOD:** Anything vegetarian

**CAN USUALLY BE FOUND:** Picking flowers

## HAMSTER

**EYE COLOR:** Bright blue

**BODY COLOR:** White

**FAVORITE ACCESSORY:** Running shoes

**LIKES:** Speed

**DISLIKES:** Lying around

**FAVORITE FOOD:** Energy bars

**CAN USUALLY BE FOUND:**
On the treadmill

# DOG

**EYE COLOR:** Baby blue

**BODY COLOR:** Golden brown

**FAVORITE ACCESSORY:** Blue flower to stick behind her ear

**LIKES:** Hangin' ten

**DISLIKES:** Wearing shoes

**FAVORITE FOOD:** Surf and turf

**CAN USUALLY BE FOUND:** Catching a wave

# CAT

**EYE COLOR:** Bright green

**BODY COLOR:** Pure white

**FAVORITE ACCESSORY:** Skateboard

**LIKES:** Scary movies

**DISLIKES:** Getting dressed up

**FAVORITE FOOD:** Popcorn

**CAN USUALLY BE FOUND:** At a double feature

# PRIM 'N' PROPER

These pets always know just how to act and how to accessorize. They're the most put-together pets in the Littlest Pet Shop, and if you're extra sweet to them, they just might teach you a thing or two!

# CAT

**EYE COLOR:** Hazel

**BODY COLOR:** White and tan

**FAVORITE ACCESSORY:** Jeweled collar

**LIKES:** A clean litter box

**DISLIKES:** Sourpusses

**FAVORITE FOOD:** Mashed potatoes

**CAN USUALLY BE FOUND:** Tidying up the house

# CAT

**EYE COLOR:** Periwinkle blue

**BODY COLOR:** Orange and white

**FAVORITE ACCESSORY:** Chic carrying case

**LIKES:** Jet-setting

**DISLIKES:** Flying coach

**FAVORITE FOOD:** Caviar

**CAN USUALLY BE FOUND:** In the first-class airport lounge

# KITTEN

**EYE COLOR:** Baby blue

**BODY COLOR:** Gray

**FAVORITE ACCESSORY:** Fancy dress

**LIKES:** Throwing parties

**DISLIKES:** Running out of snacks

**FAVORITE FOOD:** Hor d'oeuvres

**CAN USUALLY BE FOUND:** Entertaining guests

# MONKEY

**EYE COLOR:** Dark lavender

**BODY COLOR:** Light and dark tan

**FAVORITE ACCESSORY:** Leotard

**LIKES:** Gymnastics

**DISLIKES:** The balance beam

**FAVORITE FOOD:** Banana creme pie

**CAN USUALLY BE FOUND:** At the gym

## BIRD

**EYE COLOR:** Robin's egg blue

**BODY COLOR:** Light blue and yellow

**FAVORITE ACCESSORY:** Makeup kit

**LIKES:** Makeovers

**DISLIKES:** Not getting enough beauty rest

**FAVORITE FOOD:** Salad with dressing on the side

**CAN USUALLY BE FOUND:** Looking in the mirror

## BIRD

**EYE COLOR:** Violet

**BODY COLOR:** Turquoise and white

**FAVORITE ACCESSORY:** Nail file

**LIKES:** Manicures

**DISLIKES:** Hangnails

**FAVORITE FOOD:** Peeled grapes

**CAN USUALLY BE FOUND:**
Getting her nails done

# BIRD

**EYE COLOR:**
Bright blue

**BODY COLOR:**
Cotton-candy pink

**FAVORITE ACCESSORY:**
Sunscreen

**LIKES:** Catching some rays

**DISLIKES:** Getting her feathers wet

**FAVORITE FOOD:** Dried cranberries

**CAN USUALLY BE FOUND:** Lounging by the pool

# BUNNY

**EYE COLOR:** Pale lavender

**BODY COLOR:** White

**FAVORITE ACCESSORY:** Apron

**LIKES:** Baking

**DISLIKES:** Making a mess

**FAVORITE FOOD:** Peanut butter cookies

**CAN USUALLY BE FOUND:** Hopping around the kitchen

# MONKEY

**EYE COLOR:** Olive green

**BODY COLOR:** Tan and dark brown

**FAVORITE ACCESSORY:** Pink bow

**LIKES:** Secret admirers

**DISLIKES:** Working hard

**FAVORITE FOOD:** Candy hearts

**CAN USUALLY BE FOUND:** At the mall

You'll know that spring is in the air when these fun-loving pets come out to play. You can find them in a meadow, in a park, or anyplace where they can enjoy the sunshine.

# BUNNY

**EYE COLOR:** Emerald green

**BODY COLOR:** White and brown

**FAVORITE ACCESSORY:** Pink flower

**LIKES:** Looking sweet

**DISLIKES:** Scary movies

**FAVORITE FOOD:** Birthday cake

**CAN USUALLY BE FOUND:** In the sandbox

## CHIHUAHUA

**EYE COLOR:** Lavender

**BODY COLOR:** Caramel and tan

**FAVORITE ACCESSORY:** Checkered bandanna

**LIKES:** Monster trucks

**DISLIKES:** Being called "pip-squeak"

**FAVORITE FOOD:** Foot-long hot dogs

**CAN USUALLY BE FOUND:** At the auto body shop

## LADYBUG

**EYE COLOR:** Neon green

**BODY COLOR:** Red and black

**FAVORITE ACCESSORY:** Sunglasses

**LIKES:** Gardening

**DISLIKES:** Astroturf

**FAVORITE FOOD:** Fruit salad

**CAN USUALLY BE FOUND:** Sunning herself on a daisy

# BUNNY

**EYE COLOR:** Turquoise

**BODY COLOR:** Dark tan

**FAVORITE ACCESSORY:** Green sun visor

**LIKES:** Break dancing

**DISLIKES:** Ballet

**FAVORITE FOOD:** Cheese-steak sandwiches

**CAN USUALLY BE FOUND:** Busting a move

# DOG

**EYE COLOR:** Royal blue

**BODY COLOR:** Brown and white

**FAVORITE ACCESSORY:** Record player

**LIKES:** Spinning tunes

**DISLIKES:** Silence

**FAVORITE FOOD:** Cheese fries

**CAN USUALLY BE FOUND:** At the record store

## APE

**EYE COLOR:** Grass green

**BODY COLOR:** Dark brown

**FAVORITE ACCESSORY:** Yo-yo

**LIKES:** Carnivals

**DISLIKES:** Clowns

**FAVORITE FOOD:** Cotton candy

**CAN USUALLY BE FOUND:** On a roller coaster

## CAT

**EYE COLOR:** Blue

**BODY COLOR:** Gray and white

**FAVORITE ACCESSORY:** Camera

**LIKES:** Photo shoots

**DISLIKES:** Divas

**FAVORITE FOOD:** Sunflower seeds

**CAN USUALLY BE FOUND:**
In her photo studio

# BUNNY

**EYE COLOR:** Magenta

**BODY COLOR:** White and tan

**FAVORITE ACCESSORY:** Baseball bat

**LIKES:** Being a team player

**DISLIKES:** Striking out

**FAVORITE FOOD:** Peanuts

**CAN USUALLY BE FOUND:** At the ball game

# CAT

**EYE COLOR:** Lavender

**BODY COLOR:** White and gray

**FAVORITE ACCESSORY:** Helmet and knee pads

**LIKES:** Extreme sports

**DISLIKES:** Being called "princess"

**FAVORITE FOOD:** Burgers and fries

**CAN USUALLY BE FOUND:** Thrill-seeking

# FROG

**EYE COLOR:** Bright orange

**BODY COLOR:** Bright green

**FAVORITE ACCESSORY:** Visor

**LIKES:** Sunbathing

**DISLIKES:** Cold weather

**FAVORITE FOOD:** Soft-serve ice cream

**CAN USUALLY BE FOUND:** Lying on the beach

## MONKEY

**EYE COLOR:** Olive green

**BODY COLOR:** Reddish brown

**FAVORITE ACCESSORY:** Beret

**LIKES:** Painting

**DISLIKES:** Cartoons

**FAVORITE FOOD:** Crêpes suzette

**CAN USUALLY BE FOUND:** At the art museum

## DOG

**EYE COLOR:** Lavender

**BODY COLOR:** Yellow

**FAVORITE ACCESSORY:** Striped scarf

**LIKES:** Walks in the woods

**DISLIKES:** City life

**FAVORITE FOOD:** Shepherd's pie

**CAN USUALLY BE FOUND:** Curled up in front of the fireplace

## PIG

**EYE COLOR:** Periwinkle blue

**BODY COLOR:** Sandy pink

**FAVORITE ACCESSORY:** Lace bonnet

**LIKES:** Doing needlepoint

**DISLIKES:** Rock music

**FAVORITE FOOD:** Tea and cake

**CAN USUALLY BE FOUND:** In her rocking chair

## DUCK

**EYE COLOR:** Fuchsia

**BODY COLOR:** Bright yellow

**FAVORITE ACCESSORY:** Sunglasses

**LIKES:** The high diving board

**DISLIKES:** Getting out of the pool

**FAVORITE FOOD:** Vegetarian sushi

**CAN USUALLY BE FOUND:** Splashing around in the pond

## DOG

**EYE COLOR:** Violet

**BODY COLOR:** Golden brown

**FAVORITE ACCESSORY:** Frisbee

**LIKES:** Bike rides

**DISLIKES:** Wind in his ears

**FAVORITE FOOD:** Peanut butter and jelly sandwiches

**CAN USUALLY BE FOUND:** In a bike basket

## CAT

**EYE COLOR:** Bright blue

**BODY COLOR:** Gray

**FAVORITE ACCESSORY:** Purple bow

**LIKES:** Singing in the shower

**DISLIKES:** Sore throats

**FAVORITE FOOD:** Lemon poppy seed muffins

**CAN USUALLY BE FOUND:** At choir practice

## RABBIT

**EYE COLOR:** Light green

**BODY COLOR:** White

**FAVORITE ACCESSORY:** Binoculars

**LIKES:** Gardening

**DISLIKES:** Weeds

**FAVORITE FOOD:** Salad greens

**CAN USUALLY BE FOUND:** In her garden

## MOUSE

**EYE COLOR:** Turquoise

**BODY COLOR:** Pink

**FAVORITE ACCESSORY:** Pad and pencil

**LIKES:** Sketching

**DISLIKES:** Scaring people

**FAVORITE FOOD:** Ham and cheese omelets

**CAN USUALLY BE FOUND:** People-watching

# LAMB

**EYE COLOR:** Deep turquoise

**BODY COLOR:** White

**FAVORITE ACCESSORY:** Pretty pink hair bow

**LIKES:** Green pastures

**DISLIKES:** Rainy days

**FAVORITE FOOD:** Veggie burgers

**CAN USUALLY BE FOUND:** Knitting a sweater

# BUNNY

**EYE COLOR:** Light green

**BODY COLOR:** Brown and white

**FAVORITE ACCESSORY:** Woven basket

**LIKES:** Picking flowers

**DISLIKES:** Hip-hop music

**FAVORITE FOOD:** Carrot cake

**CAN USUALLY BE FOUND:** Basket weaving

# SQUEAKY CLEAN

These pets are the freshest on the block. From their fluffy fur coats to their perfectly polished paws, they love to keep themselves neat and tidy. Did someone say bath time?

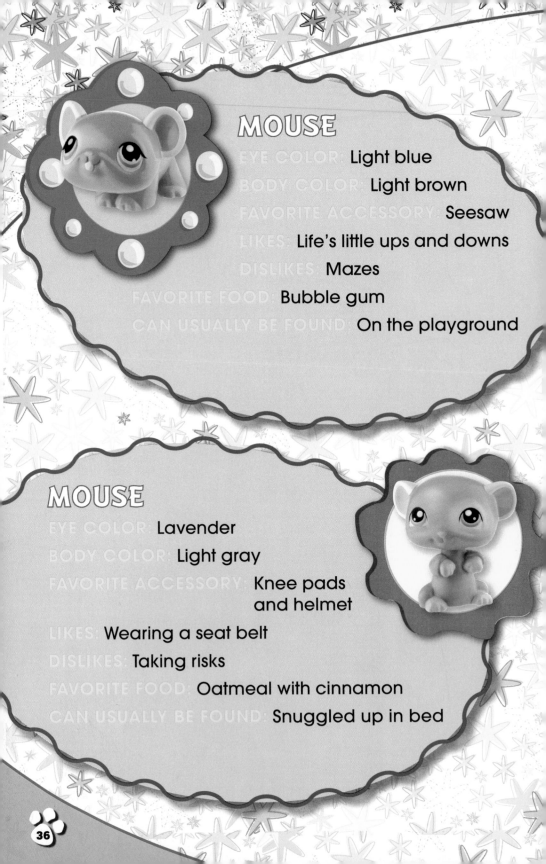

## MOUSE

EYE COLOR: Light blue

BODY COLOR: Light brown

FAVORITE ACCESSORY: Seesaw

LIKES: Life's little ups and downs

DISLIKES: Mazes

FAVORITE FOOD: Bubble gum

CAN USUALLY BE FOUND: On the playground

## MOUSE

EYE COLOR: Lavender

BODY COLOR: Light gray

FAVORITE ACCESSORY: Knee pads and helmet

LIKES: Wearing a seat belt

DISLIKES: Taking risks

FAVORITE FOOD: Oatmeal with cinnamon

CAN USUALLY BE FOUND: Snuggled up in bed

# DOG

EYE COLOR: Emerald green

BODY COLOR: Light gray

FAVORITE ACCESSORY: Chew rope

LIKES: Playing tug-of-war

DISLIKES: Letting go of the rope

FAVORITE FOOD: Licorice

CAN USUALLY BE FOUND: At the park

# CAT

EYE COLOR: Dark green

BODY COLOR: Golden brown

FAVORITE ACCESSORY: Squeaky purple toy mouse

LIKES: Chasing her tail

DISLIKES: Getting muddy

FAVORITE FOOD: Spaghetti and meatballs

CAN USUALLY BE FOUND: Watching game shows on TV

## CAT

**EYE COLOR:** Dusty blue

**BODY COLOR:** Tan

**FAVORITE ACCESSORY:** Washcloth and scrub brush

**LIKES:** Long soaks

**DISLIKES:** Getting pruney paws

**FAVORITE FOOD:** Watermelon

**CAN USUALLY BE FOUND:** In a bubble bath

## SUGAR GLIDER

**EYE COLOR:** Olive green

**BODY COLOR:** White and gray

**FAVORITE ACCESSORY:** Parachute

**LIKES:** Heights

**DISLIKES:** Having her feet planted firmly on the ground

**FAVORITE FOOD:** Acorn squash

**CAN USUALLY BE FOUND:** Soaring through the treetops

# FERRET

**EYE COLOR:** Hazel

**BODY COLOR:** Tan and brown

**FAVORITE ACCESSORY:** Light blue harness

**LIKES:** Small spaces

**DISLIKES:** Busybodies

**FAVORITE FOOD:** Saltwater taffy

**CAN USUALLY BE FOUND:** Relaxing in a hammock

# DUCK

EYE COLOR: Pale blue

BODY COLOR: Light yellow

FAVORITE ACCESSORY: Rowboat

LIKES: Getting her feet wet

DISLIKES: Getting sand in her feathers

FAVORITE FOOD: Corn on the cob

CAN USUALLY BE FOUND: Splashing around

# DOG

EYE COLOR: Ice blue

BODY COLOR: Tan and white

FAVORITE ACCESSORY: Fishing rod

LIKES: Catching a big one

DISLIKES: The ones that get away

FAVORITE FOOD: Fresh fish

CAN USUALLY BE FOUND: At the lake

# SUMMERTIME PAL

The temperature may be rising, but this pet doesn't mind. She knows how to keep cool even in the hottest weather. Take her to the beach or on a picnic and enjoy the lazy days of summer together!

# HUMMINGBIRD

**EYE COLOR:** Deep green

**BODY COLOR:** Green

**FAVORITE ACCESSORY:** Sunglasses

**LIKES:** Fresh flowers

**DISLIKES:** Smog

**FAVORITE FOOD:** Jelly beans

**CAN USUALLY BE FOUND:** At the candy store

Sweeter than a candy-coated gumdrop, these pets are guaranteed to put a smile on your face!

# CHIPMUNK

**EYE COLOR:** Olive green

**BODY COLOR:** Brown and white

**FAVORITE ACCESSORY:** Nutcracker

**LIKES:** Scampering

**DISLIKES:** Shells in her bed

**FAVORITE FOOD:** Peanut brittle

**CAN USUALLY BE FOUND:**
Making funny faces in the mirror

# RACCOON

**EYE COLOR:** Pale blue

**BODY COLOR:** Gray and black

**FAVORITE ACCESSORY:** Chef's hat and apron

**LIKES:** Cooking

**DISLIKES:** Being hungry

**FAVORITE FOOD:** Dessert

**CAN USUALLY BE FOUND:**
Saying, "Kiss the cook!"

# BUMBLEBEE

**EYE COLOR:** Neon blue

**BODY COLOR:** Yellow and black

**FAVORITE ACCESSORY:** Honeycomb

**LIKES:** Being queen bee

**DISLIKES:** Having sticky fingers

**FAVORITE FOOD:** Sugar cookies

**CAN USUALLY BE FOUND:** In the flower shop

# BUTTERFLY

**EYE COLOR:** Light purple

**BODY COLOR:** Pink and yellow

**FAVORITE ACCESSORY:** Ballet shoes

**LIKES:** Dancing

**DISLIKES:** Football

**FAVORITE FOOD:** Pastries

**CAN USUALLY BE FOUND:** Practicing her pirouettes

## GUINEA PIG

**EYE COLOR:** Dark olive green

**BODY COLOR:** Cream and tan

**FAVORITE ACCESSORY:**
Reading glasses

**LIKES:** Reading the dictionary

**DISLIKES:** Television

**FAVORITE FOOD:** Artichokes

**CAN USUALLY BE FOUND:** Curled up with
a good book

## TURTLE

**EYE COLOR:** Light blue

**BODY COLOR:** Light green

**FAVORITE ACCESSORY:** Ski hat

**LIKES:** Playing chess

**DISLIKES:** Highways

**FAVORITE FOOD:** Well-done steak

**CAN USUALLY BE FOUND:**
Taking his time

# CAT

**EYE COLOR:** Olive green

**BODY COLOR:** White and tan

**FAVORITE ACCESSORY:** Scissors

**LIKES:** Styling her friends' hair

**DISLIKES:** Bad perms

**FAVORITE FOOD:** Potato chips

**CAN USUALLY BE FOUND:** At her hair salon

# CAT

**EYE COLOR:** Bright blue

**BODY COLOR:** Cream

**FAVORITE ACCESSORY:** Cordless phone

**LIKES:** Juicy gossip

**DISLIKES:** Reading the newspaper

**FAVORITE FOOD:** Pretzels

**CAN USUALLY BE FOUND:** Talking on the phone

# DOG

**EYE COLOR:** Dark brown

**BODY COLOR:** White and brown

**FAVORITE ACCESSORY:** Magnifying glass

**LIKES:** Catching the culprit

**DISLIKES:** Crime

**FAVORITE FOOD:** Stinky cheese

**CAN USUALLY BE FOUND:** Sniffing out clues

# POODLE

**EYE COLOR:** Violet

**BODY COLOR:** Pink

**FAVORITE ACCESSORY:** Spiked collar

**LIKES:** Punk rock

**DISLIKES:** Classical music

**FAVORITE FOOD:** Pizza

**CAN USUALLY BE FOUND:** Playing drums with her band

# SCOTTIE

**EYE COLOR:** Violet

**BODY COLOR:** White

**FAVORITE ACCESSORY:** Bagpipes

**LIKES:** Plaid

**DISLIKES:** Wearing knits

**FAVORITE FOOD:** Shortbread

**CAN USUALLY BE FOUND:** At a parade

# VALENTINE PETS

Every day is Valentine's Day with these pets. They're super cuddly, and they live to love. Give them a heart-shaped box of candy and they'll be yours forever.

# POODLE

**EYE COLOR:**
Light purple

**BODY COLOR:**
White and gray

**FAVORITE ACCESSORY:** Purple bow

**LIKES:** Romance novels

**DISLIKES:** Loud noises

**FAVORITE FOOD:** Rice pudding

**CAN USUALLY BE FOUND:** In the library

# KITTEN

**EYE COLOR:** Olive green

**BODY COLOR:** Light brown

**FAVORITE ACCESSORY:** Soft and
cuddly cat bed

**LIKES:** Staying indoors

**DISLIKES:** Bad weather

**FAVORITE FOOD:** Pizza bagels

**CAN USUALLY BE FOUND:** Curled up by
the fireplace

# BIRD

**EYE COLOR:** Dark purple

**BODY COLOR:** Yellow, green, and white

**FAVORITE ACCESSORY:** Telescope

**LIKES:** Stargazing

**DISLIKES:** Clouds

**FAVORITE FOOD:** Astronaut ice cream

**CAN USUALLY BE FOUND:** Looking at the night sky

# BUNNY

**EYE COLOR:** Neon blue

**BODY COLOR:** Golden brown

**FAVORITE ACCESSORY:** Barrettes

**LIKES:** Opening fortune cookies

**DISLIKES:** Mean people

**FAVORITE FOOD:** Alfalfa sprouts

**CAN USUALLY BE FOUND:** Tie-dyeing her socks

# PIG

**EYE COLOR:** Lime green

**BODY COLOR:** Pink

**FAVORITE ACCESSORY:** Headband

**LIKES:** Exercising

**DISLIKES:** Sleeping through the alarm

**FAVORITE FOOD:** Anything spicy

**CAN USUALLY BE FOUND:** At the gym

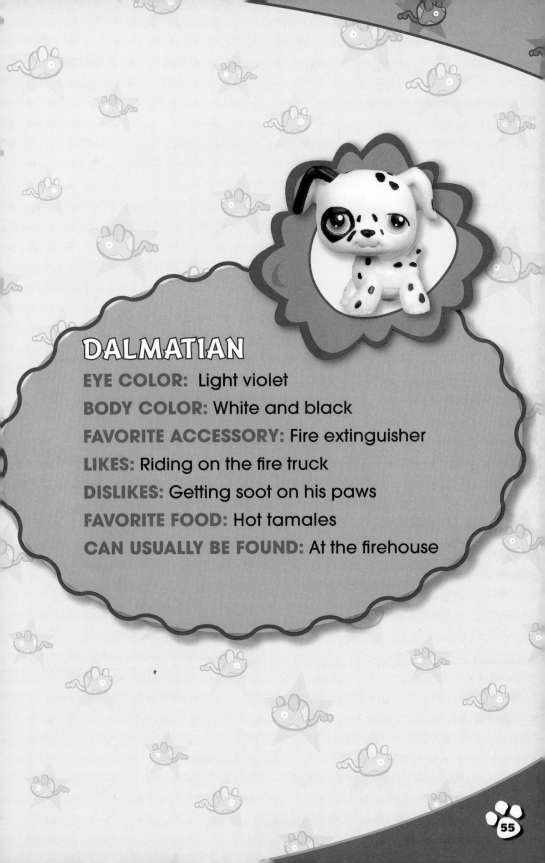

# DALMATIAN

**EYE COLOR:** Light violet

**BODY COLOR:** White and black

**FAVORITE ACCESSORY:** Fire extinguisher

**LIKES:** Riding on the fire truck

**DISLIKES:** Getting soot on his paws

**FAVORITE FOOD:** Hot tamales

**CAN USUALLY BE FOUND:** At the firehouse

# WINTERTIME PALS

BRRR...Get out your scarf and mittens 'cause you've got to bundle up to play with these pets! They love to frolic in the snow, but when it's time to come inside, give them a mug of hot apple cider and they'll become cozy critters!

## HUSKIE

**EYE COLOR:** Orange

**BODY COLOR:** Dark gray and white

**FAVORITE ACCESSORY:** Pink scarf

**LIKES:** Going sledding

**DISLIKES:** When people tell him to "mush"

**FAVORITE FOOD:** Baked Alaska

**CAN USUALLY BE FOUND:** Speeding downhill

## PANDA

**EYE COLOR:** Light green

**BODY COLOR:** Black and white

**FAVORITE ACCESSORY:** Black belt

**LIKES:** Reading the newspaper

**DISLIKES:** Getting tickled

**FAVORITE FOOD:** Ramen noodles

**CAN USUALLY BE FOUND:** Practicing karate

# DOG

**EYE COLOR:** Bright turquoise

**BODY COLOR:** Sandy brown

**FAVORITE ACCESSORY:** Blue scarf

**LIKES:** Ice-skating

**DISLIKES:** Having frizzy ears

**FAVORITE FOOD:** Warm milk

**CAN USUALLY BE FOUND:** On the frozen pond

# GRAY CAT

**EYE COLOR:** Ice blue

**BODY COLOR:** Soft gray

**FAVORITE ACCESSORY:** Striped hat

**LIKES:** Making snow pets

**DISLIKES:** Cold paws

**FAVORITE FOOD:** Corn chowder

**CAN USUALLY BE FOUND:** Throwing snowballs

# BUNNY

**EYE COLOR:** Dark green

**BODY COLOR:** Light yellow and white

**FAVORITE ACCESSORY:** Striped hat

**LIKES:** Downhill skiing

**DISLIKES:** Chapped lips

**FAVORITE FOOD:** Toasted marshmallows

**CAN USUALLY BE FOUND:** On the bunny slope

# BROWN MOUSE

**EYE COLOR:** Lavender

**BODY COLOR:** Sandy brown

**FAVORITE ACCESSORY:** Bunny slippers

**LIKES:** Slumber parties

**DISLIKES:** Monster movies

**FAVORITE FOOD:** Cheesecake

**CAN USUALLY BE FOUND:** Playing truth or dare

# PORTABLE PETS

These pets will travel with you wherever you go! Just pack them in their adorable traveling cases and hit the road!

# CHINCHILLA

**EYE COLOR:** Lavender

**BODY COLOR:** Cocoa brown

**FAVORITE ACCESSORY:** Carrying case

**LIKES:** Adventure travel

**DISLIKES:** Weather delays

**FAVORITE FOOD:** Energy bars

**CAN USUALLY BE FOUND:** Seeing the sights

# BASSET HOUND

**EYE COLOR:** Lime green

**BODY COLOR:** Caramel brown

**FAVORITE ACCESSORY:** Passport

**LIKES:** Visiting Europe

**DISLIKES:** Jet lag

**FAVORITE FOOD:** Salted peanuts

**CAN USUALLY BE FOUND:**
In first class

# How big is your Littlest Pet Shop?
## Check 'em out!

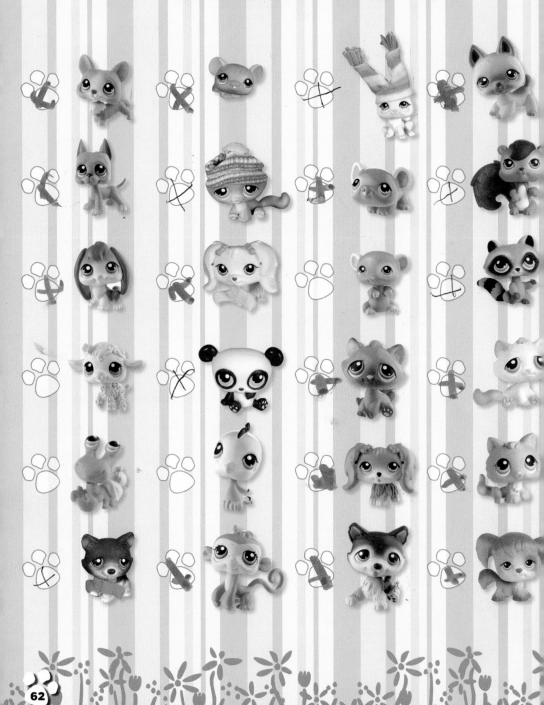

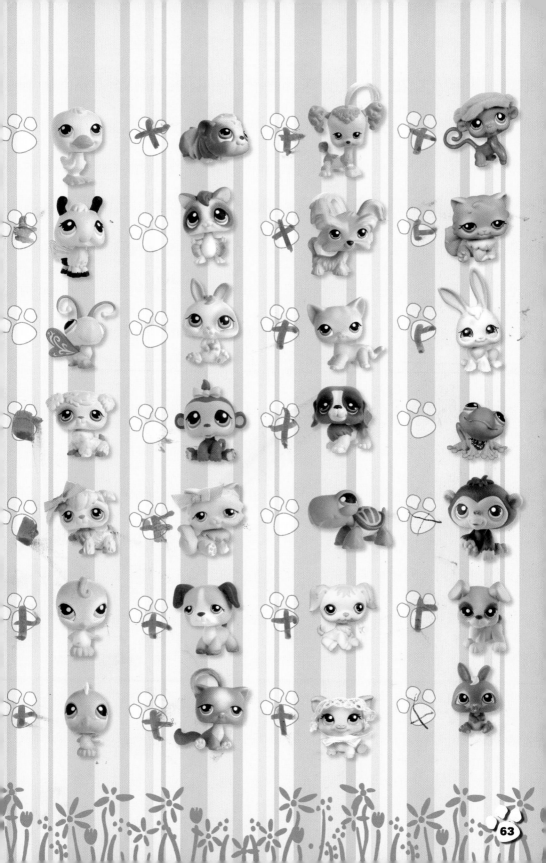